Good People Get Burned Too

Good People Get Burned Too

Eileen E. Lantry

Pacific Press Publishing Association
Mountain View, California   Oshawa, Ontario

Cover photo by Joan Walter

Copyright © 1984 by
Pacific Press Publishing Association
Printed in United States of America

Library of Congress Cataloging in Publication Data

Lantry, Eileen E.
   Good people get burned too.

   1. Lee, Rose. 2. Christian biography—United States. 3. Nurses—United
States—Biography. I. Title.
BR1725.L36L36   1984   280'.4'0924 [B]   83-21940
ISBN 0-8163-0549-8

Dedicated to my friend
Dee Thorman
who, while struggling with cancer,
clings with patience and faith
to God's promises, thus inspiring
me with my lesser problems

Contents

Chapter 1

I will be her witness. Rose Lee, ward assistant, nursing service, knew loneliness and hurt. True, her loneliness wasn't like the divorcée's sitting alone in her apartment, isolated, and full of poignant and painful memories. She never agonized under the consuming anguish felt by the young widow who often stared at pictures of happy togetherness, remembering, hurting. But she knew the desolate feeling of living under constant condemnation, even though her words and acts were motivated by unselfish love.

In her work at the hospital she saw loneliness strike the young as well as the old. She cried inside with the disillusioned teenage girl, far from home and heavy with child. She waited as the cab driver pulled the pain-wracked girl from the taxi. Hurrying her to the delivery room, she wished she knew the answer to her cry, "How can I face tomorrow alone?"

And how did she cope with her own brand of loneliness? Was there something, anything she could do to conquer this terrible enemy?

I witnessed Rose's struggle. I have rejoiced with her advancements and cried at her setbacks. But through it all I think I can hear God saying, "Be faithful, even to the point of death, and I will give you the crown of life." Revelation 2:10, NIV.

Rose Lee hurried toward the elevator. She glanced at her watch as she reached out to press the elevator button: 6:40. Hearing quick steps, she turned to look. A nurse rushed in front of her.

"Good morning," Rose said with a smile.

Without so much as turning the blond nurse grunted a meaningless "Hi" and pushed ahead of her toward the opening elevator door. Instead of following her, Rose stepped back into the corridor and watched the automatic door close.

Instantly the words she and her husband, Andrew, had memorized an hour before flashed into her mind, "This is the day the Lord has made; let us rejoice and be glad in it." Psalm 118:24, NIV.

"But, God, how can I rejoice when they don't even treat me like a person?" Rose thought. "If only they'd try to understand my poor English and accept me as one who can think and feel like they do. It's not the extra work they push on me that matters, but I do so need a friend who cares."

Frustration and resentment filled her whole being. Instead of taking the elevator she turned to the stairway and ran up the three flights of stairs. Hot tears filled her eyes. Before she opened the door to the corridor, she stopped and said, "God, You know we've only been in America a few months, but we're so used to people, lots of people around us. These Americans leave us alone. They don't seem to care. I'm so thankful for Andrew and the children, but why do I feel rejected by everybody else? Please help me!"

As Rose walked down the hall, she thought of the contrast between the Chinese and American ways of life. In Asia, families lived close, with in-laws, aunts, uncles, cousins, grandparents sharing small quarters. Now she, Andrew, and their three children lived alone in a house that seemed large and lonely to them. How they missed the fellowship of their relatives and friends!

When Rose approached the nursing station on the orthopedic ward, fourth floor east, the same blond nurse looked up. She held out a sheet of paper and said in a cold, commanding way, "Here are your orders from the charge nurse. Before you begin passing out water to the rooms, check the patient in traction in 361. You may need to release the tension."

Rose knew the proper procedure, but as a ward assistant, the law forbade her to do nurse's work. Before Rose could respond, the blond nurse slipped into a nearby room for her morning coffee.

The struggle in Rose's mind intensified. Why did the other nurses take advantage of her when the charge nurse was absent? True, they knew she was a graduate nurse from a hospital in Hong Kong, but they also knew that she had not yet taken the state boards, which would qualify her to be a registered nurse in the United States.

As Rose checked the patient in traction, she noted her pale, pain-wracked face. The patient listlessly opened her eyes. Rose sensed her misery and longed to ease her suffering. Patting the bony hand, she said, "I can't take away your pain, but I do care. I'm sorry you're hurting."

"I had a terrible night. I thought the long hours would never end."

"Is there anything I can do to bring you comfort or relief?"

"Maybe there is. Several times in the night I thought of when I was sick as a child and my mother prayed for me. Just thinking about God helped. Then the cleaning lady told me how much your prayers have helped other patients. Would you pray for me?"

"I'd be happy to." Rose took the hot hand in hers. "Dear God, this dear lady hurts so much. All night she's longed for rest. You love her. You feel her pain too. Touch her with Your healing power. In the name of Jesus, give her peace and comfort. Thank You so much. Amen."

The patient smiled weakly.

"Strange, but when you mentioned the name of Jesus, I seemed to relax. Is there some kind of power in His name?"

"I'm sure there is. Many times I've made requests in His name and He's supplied my needs. He promised never to leave us nor forsake us."

At that moment a voice on the loudspeaker called, "Rose Lee, room 340. Rose Lee, room 340."

"If only I had time to help the patients," she thought as she hurried down the hall. Suddenly she became aware that the hurt inside didn't hurt as much. Had God already begun to answer her prayer on the stairway landing? Puzzled by the warm feeling that engulfed her, she wondered where the lonely ache had gone. She must tell Andrew. Dear Andrew, so kind and understanding.

All during her busy day she helped nurses make beds and lift patients. She carried messages to hospital records, hurried with reports to doctor's offices, took specimens to the laboratory, wheeled patients to be x-rayed. Yet, even as she rushed from place to place running errands throughout the large hospital, thoughts of long ago flashed into her mind.

Loneliness at the hospital awakened memories of her childhood in Singapore. As long as she could remember, she had lived with loneliness. Maybe her search to find a way to conquer this hurt began when she realized her parents didn't want this second girl born to them. She remembered the awful feeling of rejection when she overheard her aunt tell a neighbor that her own mother gave her to a servant girl when she was only a few days old. She learned then, for the first time, that this aunt had demanded she return the baby. She felt again the pain when her aunt said, "It was my duty to be her foster mother." She then began to understand that she had never been wanted.

She knew why her family openly laughed and said, "Why bother to teach her? She's so skinny and small; she couldn't learn in school."

So Rose roamed with the neighborhood children, playing in the dirty yards. She seldom came home except to eat and sleep. If only someone had cared enough to show her love and acceptance.

Maybe that's why when she was eight, she became intrigued with the worship of the monkey god in a house-turned-temple not far from hers. One day Rose decided to peek in the door from which came the din of clashing gongs and pounding drums. Along with others she watched the spirit medium writhe in frantic dancing, slashing his tongue with a sword. She saw the dripping blood fall on specially prepared green and yellow papers covered with Chinese characters. She was fascinated as she listened to him shout from his hypnotic trance.

"Come. Be healed. Buy the papers. Burn them and drink the ashes. Bathe in them. You'll be cured from cancer, from mental trouble, from all kinds of sickness."

But many of the worshipers could not understand the complicated instructions that the spirit medium gave, for in Singapore people speak many dialects of the Chinese language. He needed a translator.

Because Rose believed that he must be helping those who came for a cure, she wanted to have a part in this mysterious healing power. Growing up playing with boys and girls who spoke these dialects, she had learned to understand them all. Though she longed to translate the words, she felt shy and afraid.

Every day this tiny black-haired girl stood to one side. No one noticed her; no one cared. One day a crippled man hobbled by her. She watched him pull his money from his pocket. She saw the sad look in his eyes as he held it up and pointed to the papers, then to his crippled legs. The spirit medium began to ask questions and explain, but the old man kept shaking his head. Finally with tears of despair, he turned away.

Rose felt his hurt. She had understood what the spirit medium had said. Rushing to the crippled man, she grabbed his bony hand.

"Please. I can help you. I know the words. I will pray to the monkey god for you. He will give the spirit medium a message for you, and I can tell you what he said."

And so the lonely little girl began to reach out to those even more lonely than she was. But sometimes the messages she translated hurt instead of helped.

She cried when she had to translate the medium's words to a poor widow. "Your baby is sick because your brother hates you. He's cast a curse on the baby. The spirits say your child will die unless you pay $100 to stop the curse."

Why, she wondered, did the spirits demand money from this poor woman who had none? Why did they send her messages of fear, hate, and despair, when people needed healing, comfort, and love? Was there no way that others, like her, could be free from the consuming anguish that bound them?

Chapter 2

Five mornings a week Rose left home early. She always stopped to peek into the bedrooms at her three sleeping children, the real reasons why the Lees had chosen to come to America. Andrew, her husband, an employee of a successful business in Hong Kong, now worked for his brother-in-law doing mechanical drawing, a job below his ability. After she would leave, he usually supervised breakfast and getting-ready-for-school preparations.

She smiled at her firstborn, twelve-year-old Joseph, whose chronic asthma and bronchitis had greatly improved in a drier climate. Pretty, quiet Yvette—how she hated to put so many burdens on her eleven-year-old shoulders. And then, Johnny, her baby, now almost eight. She regretted she'd missed much of his babyhood. She often wondered if the sacrifice to begin nurse's training shortly after his birth had been worth the loss.

Had they made a mistake coming to America to get a good education for these children they loved so much? She recalled the callous treatment they received at the U.S. embassy, the endless questions that made them feel like outcasts. All doors to immigration seemed closed. They prayed God's will be done. Then the situation changed. A relative paid their air fare. Andrew's sister provided a home in Denver. Andrew found work, and she was hired as ward assistant with the promise that she could begin studying to take her state boards.

Months had passed since she and her family had arrived in

America. Still she felt alone, different, strange, insecure. If only people would speak to her at the supermarket or welcome her family at church as if they belonged. How she longed for a genuine, friendly "Hello, I'm glad you're here."

But in spite of being ignored, Rose felt compelled to reach out, to smile, to care.

"God," she prayed, "I need someone in my life with whom I can share Your love. Help me to find joy like Jesus did."

That same day the nurses got behind in their work. One of them asked her to begin Tom's morning bath. A teenage boy, he lay mangled and torn from a motorcyle accident.

"Hi, Tom," said Rose, "sorry the nurses left you till last."

"Guess I'll always be last from now on," he grumbled. "Seems like nobody cares about me."

"I doubt that." Rose turned so she could look straight at him. "I grew up a loner, certain that no one cared about me. But I found out I was wrong."

"How?" he asked.

"Had a very unusual dream. I believe God gave it to me."

"Come on," Tom sneered, "you can't tell me God's that interested in people."

"Well, I could if you wanted to listen, but I didn't come in here to bore you."

"What's there to do? These broken legs have got me grounded. Go on, let's hear what you've got to say."

Rose directed a prayer heavenward as she began preparations for his bath.

"As a kid I believed that the spirits could cure all kinds of sicknesses. One day after I had started school, a friend told me of another God. She said He had magic powers even greater than the spirits.

"I got interested right away. This friend took me to a different kind of school, one that met only on Sunday morning. I didn't tell my parents. I can't remember what the teacher said, but I never forgot the picture in that room."

Rose went to the foot of the patient's bed.

"I saw a Man dressed in a long, white robe, surrounded by small, white animals such as I had never seen. They didn't look like the mangy dogs and scrawny cats or the huge rats that fought for food in Singapore's alleys where I lived. Pressing close to this man, these animals looked up at the baby animal He held in His arms. The kind, loving look in that Man's eyes fascinated me. The teacher said He loved animals, but He loved children more. She told us of His power to heal sick folks, but what captivated me most was the way He loved."

Tom interrupted, "Are you describing that picture of Jesus, where He's supposed to be some shepherd with a bunch of sheep?"

"Right." Rose began to change the sheets as she talked. "You see I'd never heard of Jesus nor of heaven. Worship to me meant offering incense, burning paper money, bringing food to appease the terrible power of the spirits. I lived in fear of their curses. My gods hated both animals and children.

"I wondered how this God's power differed from the ones I had known. I was too shy to ask questions. How could a god be kind and loving as well as powerful?"

Rose paused, noting the thoughtful look on the boy's face.

"One night when I was nine years old, I dreamed I had gone for a walk down a wide road. Suddenly I saw a beautiful light glowing on a narrow path hardly wide enough for my feet. I followed the brilliant glow, gazing in wonder around me. No dirty gutters filled with rotting garbage, no rubbish like that which cluttered the crowded streets of Singapore. The path led through green fields dotted with colorful flowers. I stopped to listen to the birds singing from the trees. And then I saw the animals, white and clean, running toward a Man with a robe even whiter. In one hand He held a long, curved stick, and in the other cuddled a baby animal.

"Suddenly I remembered the picture at Sunday School. Could this be the God-man, Jesus, who loved and cared for children and sheep? He looked at me with His kind eyes and smiled. I'd never felt such happiness. I began to run toward Him shouting, 'Are you Jesus? I'm here! I'm coming!' At that moment I awoke."

"What a dream!" Tom exclaimed.

"But what a disappointment to a little girl who wanted to get acquainted with the Man who had kind eyes and a loving smile. I lay on my cot wondering what it all meant, whether I'd ever know and understand. I could think of nothing else!

"The next morning I determined to talk to this God-man, the way I had seen the teacher do at Sunday School. I knelt beside my cot. Just as I folded my hands and shut my eyes, my Buddhist uncle came into the room."

"Rose," he shouted, "where did you learn to do that?" He yanked me to my feet and demanded, "Have you gone to a Christian church?"

"I was too scared to talk, so I just nodded my head.

"He dragged me to my parents, slapping me repeatedly. They wouldn't allow me out of their sight on Sunday mornings after that."

By this time Rose had finished her work. She paused at the door of Tom's room.

"Tom, many years passed before I learned that Jesus, too, lived a lonely life. That no one on earth understood Him. That no one really appreciated Him, not even His mother, His brothers, nor His disciples. And when I discovered that He did all this because He loved me, that my sins forced Him to be lonely, separated from His Father, it broke my heart."

Tom looked surprised. "You mean Jesus is lonely too?"

The voice on the loudspeaker interrupted. "Rose Lee, nursing station. Rose Lee, nursing station."

Chapter 3

When Rose brought fresh ice water to Tom later in the day drops of cold sweat stood out on his forehead. Rose noticed the struggle he was having trying to turn himself in bed and her heart went out to him in sympathy.

"Your leg is hurting pretty bad, isn't it?" she said as she helped him turn over on his side.

"Sure does," Tom groaned. "Last week I was the best track runner on our team. Today I struggled five minutes to move my leg two inches. He paused, then added bitterly, "Tomorrow you'll be pushing me in a wheelchair to therapy to learn to wiggle my toes."

Rose smiled sympathetically as she sensed his despair and laid her hand on his cast.

"Tom, I'm sorry for your hurt and disappointment. I remember how it feels to be young and left alone, unable to keep up with your friends."

"Really? Were you an accident victim too?"

"Not a sudden victim like you, but the victim of ugly circumstances that left me far behind others my own age. But now, years later, though I wouldn't choose the pain again, I am grateful for what that pain has taught me."

"Rose, you talk in circles. You don't make any sense."

"And I can't explain now. They keep me too busy! But, if you wish, I could come by when I'm off duty."

"Would you?" Tom grinned broadly. "I'll promise not to run away," he added impishly.

Shortly after three o'clock Rose walked into his room and dropped into a chair.

"Mind if I sit down? I'm tired!"

"No wonder. I hear them paging you every few minutes. Don't they ever give you a break?"

"I get a break at lunchtime. But that's OK. When I serve so many patients who can't walk, I'm glad that I have two legs and that my feet can move fast."

Tom looked at his legs encased in casts, then at Rose. "And how can this mess ever make me feel grateful?"

"Maybe I should tell you of my unhappy teenage years before we talk about that."

"Sure, misery loves company." Tom relaxed on his pillows.

"When my folks did allow me to go to school," Rose continued, "most of the other children were years younger than I. At first I felt so eager to learn, I didn't care about the age difference. But after three years, I knew I didn't belong. I hoped that by transferring to an English-speaking school, I'd fit in better. But I didn't know one word of English. So they put me into the first grade. Uncaring teachers gave me little help, as a result I progressed slowly. At sixteen, because of my poor English, they denied me entrance into the overcrowded secondary schools. I discovered that private schools wouldn't accept me either. I made daily trips to the temple to ask the gods to solve my problem. But that didn't help a bit. It's awful, Tom, to feel unaccepted and of little worth."

"You sure had a tough break," Tom muttered. "Wasn't there any school that you could go to?"

"Someone told me of a church-operated school on the far side of Singapore island that might accept overage students. I begged my mother to allow me to apply. Grudgingly she gave me the bus fare. I felt scared, unsure, but desperate. When I asked to enroll, instead of rejecting me, they explained I could attend if I promised to abide by the Christian rules of the school. When I heard the word *Christian*, memories flooded my brain. Instantly I thought of the God-man of my dream.''

"Didn't your mom know the school was Christian?" Tom interrupted.

"Yes. For hours she warned me of the evils of Christian nonsense. But when I pointed out that if I improved my English I could qualify for a higher paying job, she consented to pay my school fees.

"Did you like that school?"

"Yes. Many of the kids were overage like me. But the real breakthrough began in Bible class. There I discovered that God made this world. I heard stories of people who found a way out of life's messes. People like Abraham, Joseph, and Moses. Tom, can you imagine my excitement when I heard the whole story of Jesus from Bethlehem to Calvary? It kept me awake at night, as I tried to piece together this puzzle of a God who loved people so much He gave His life for them. Can you understand my confusion as I shifted from gods I could see, even if they didn't care, to an unseen God who did care?"

"Not really. I guess those Sunday School stories have become old stuff to me. But how did you get along with your English?"

"My English improved because of my interest in Bible study. The hard words forced me to use the Chinese-English dictionary. In Singapore students have to attend school six days a week. So, on Saturday morning I joined my new friends at what they called Sabbath School and church."

Tom chuckled, as he said, "At least you put one over on your mother. But what's all this got to do with being grateful?"

"Well, let me explain. I learned that God loved me personally. I believed He cared about my troubles. I wanted to love Him too. But how? I had so many fears. Would He accept me when others rejected me? Why should He? I had nothing to offer! Yet I wanted to belong to Him. Soon Chinese New Year was coming. How was I supposed to please this new God?"

"What's so special about Chinese New Year?" Tom asked.

"The Chinese celebrate for two weeks. The most important

celebration comes on the ninth day. Every member of the family gathers around the altar in the living room to worship. They believe their offering must please their god, or the spirits will cause curses, sickness, trouble, or even death during the coming year. For weeks I struggled with this. I couldn't offer joss sticks [a stick covered with powdered sandlewood and burned by the Chinese as incense] and food to an idol, because I now believed in the Creator-God.''

''What did you do?''

''I stood back watching, repeating in my mind, 'Thou shalt have no other gods before me. . . . Thou shalt not bow down thyself to them, nor serve them' [Exodus 20:3-5]. Seeing my reluctance, my mother put the food in my hand and pulled me to the altar saying, 'All my children must worship the gods.' She was a large woman, and her strong grasp on my arm hurt. Even though I was scared, I shook my head, laid the food on the table, and said, 'I cannot.' ''

''I'll bet that made her mad.''

''It surely did. She got so angry she knocked me to the floor with one blow. Then she began kicking me with her bare feet. My foster brother joined her. Shouting curses, they dragged me into another room. Then, because they feared that my refusal to worship would make the spirits angry, my whole family kicked and hit me. Lying face down, I buried my head in my arms to protect my face. I had mixed feelings—I felt guilt because I'd spoiled their worship, but joy in my decision to follow the true God. Although I experienced the hatred of my family, I had a peace and acceptance that even Mother's final threat did not disturb, when she yelled, 'If you won't worship the gods, I will stop paying your school fees.' ''

''Did you report your injuries to the police?''

''No. In my country Chinese custom is that children must obey their parents. Kids usually don't do what I did.''

''Did she follow through with her threat?'' Tom asked.

''Not until some time later.''

Rose glanced at her watch. ''Tom, I'd like to tell you more, but I must go home and fix supper for my family.''

She stepped close to his bed and took his hand.

"Believe me, Tom, knowing Jesus has made a great deal of difference to me. Jesus knows about your hurt legs too, and He cares. In the Good Shepherd picture, Jesus is carrying the lamb because it has a broken leg. If you'll just trust Him and believe His promises, you'll find the pain easier to bear. He'll give you joy that even suffering can't take away."

"But I don't know any promises."

"That's why I wrote out a couple of promises just for you. Will you take them?" She laid a piece of paper on his bedside stand and left.

Tom stared out the door at the empty hall for several minutes. Then he reached for the paper and read what it said:

Jesus promised:

I will never leave you nor forsake you.
Lo, I am with you alway, even unto the end of the world.

Chapter 4

Rose had the weekend off, so she didn't see Tom the next day.

Being with her family gave her a sense of relief. Here she didn't have to see the pain, the hurt, and the helplessness of those who were suffering and sick. Worshiping God in church seemed to her an opportunity to listen for ideas that might help the patients. The minister's first words got her attention.

"If anyone had reason to feel on top of the world, it was Elijah. Yet, soon after his great triumph on Mount Carmel, the prophet fell so low that he asked God to let him die. After his signal victory over the prophets of Baal, he ran away to hide in the desert. Where had his faith and hope gone? Emotionally and physically drained, he felt an overpowering loneliness. In despair he thought he had no future. For three and a half years his name had topped the list of the most-wanted criminals in Israel. Yet he had lived without fear. What happened to make him prefer death?"

Rose felt that the minister was speaking directly to her. "Notice how God dealt with His lonely, despondent prophet. First, He had to get his attention. Elijah's thoughts had turned inward. He had taken his eyes off God and placed them on himself. When he quit depending on God, fear drove him into hiding.

"Sometimes God has to treat us like He did Elijah. He allows tragedies, emotional or physical cyclones, troubles that seem like earthquakes and fires to get our attention too. When we are willing to listen, then God gets gentle and whispers, 'What are you doing here so far from Me?' "

Rose leaned forward. She needed every word.

"Watch how God pointed out the trouble spots in Elijah's life. He said, 'You've been trying to do My job, Elijah. I can take care of Jezebel and her gang. I only asked you to bring glory to My name. No wonder you got discouraged and depressed. You overdid both physically and emotionally. In your frustration, you came to wrong conclusions. You thought you were the only one faithful to Me. But, Elijah, I have 7000 loyal and true followers left in Israel that you don't know anything about.

" 'Let's get down to basics—your real problem. You didn't depend on Me. You didn't trust Me. If only you'd remembered I'm still in charge; if you'd trusted My infinite power, you'd never be out here wallowing in despair.' "

The preacher paused and smiled.

"I can imagine God putting His arms around Elijah, holding him close, and saying, 'My son, forget yourself. Quit licking your wounds. Instead of feeling sorry for yourself, go back to work. Get involved. Reach out to others, but keep your focus on Me. I'll help you do the important jobs I've planned for you. You'll succeed, too, if you depend on Me.' "

The minister finished, but Rose's mind raced back to the time in her life when she first learned to depend on God.

Then she thought of Tom. Maybe he could face his future better if she shared with him her hurts and triumphs, her victories and heartaches.

She decided to go see Tom on Sunday after visiting hours.

"Sure nice of you to drop by," Tom remarked.

"Couldn't stop thinking of you and your pain. Thought maybe you might sleep better after a bedtime story," Rose said with a laugh.

"I'm more used to a late movie. Do you have a thriller?" Tom grinned.

"You'll have to be the judge of that. Let me tell you what happened when I started to live out what I read in the Bible," Rose answered.

"One day at dinner my mother confronted me. 'You've always

enjoyed pork and prawns, but lately I've seen you pick them out and throw them away. Why don't you eat them anymore?'

" 'Mother,' I explained, 'in God's book, the Bible, He says that we shouldn't eat pork. It is not good for us. So I'd rather eat eggs with my vegetables.'

" 'Is that so! Very well! I'll see about that!' she threatened. 'If you won't eat the food I provide, then you'll eat only rice and eggs.'

"The next few weeks of nothing but white rice and eggs were awful! I longed for the many fresh fruits of the tropics. That week in Bible class we read the story of the manna God provided for Israel in the wilderness. This gave me an idea. Couldn't God keep me healthy eating just white rice?"

"How could you stand that monotonous diet?" Tom asked. "This hospital food is bad enough, but rice every day; I couldn't stand it!"

"Only God helped me endure those weeks. What I really wanted was for Him to soften my mother's heart. I wondered why He didn't deal with the really big problem. Instead, my mother became more hostile. She'd save washing, ironing, and cleaning to be done when I returned from school. As I began to get behind in my homework, I felt like rebelling."

"I'd have left home if my mom had treated me like that," Tom interrupted.

"But I couldn't. One night I cried to God. It's too much for me! You take over. To my surprise, He did! He took away my resentment toward my mother. He kept me healthy, and I got my homework done faster. A month later my mother began to give me good food again."

"You mean you gave up and let God take control of things?" Tom asked.

"Right. It's like having a close friendship with a fabulous Person. But I wanted more time to get to know Him, and I had no time. Then I found this promise, 'He wakens me morning by morning, wakens my ear like one being taught' [Isaiah 50:4, NIV]. So I asked God to be my alarm clock!"

"What? You're nuts! God's not like that!"

"Oh yes He is! He knows it takes time to get acquainted with Jesus. And the only time I had was early each morning. I never knew what awakened me. Maybe God sent an angel to touch me whispering, 'Rose, wake up. Jesus is waiting.'"

Tom looked incredulous. "Well that beats me!" he mumbled. "So what did you do?"

Rose opened her Bible and took out a small card. "It's easy, Tom. We talk, just like you and I do. I tell Him everything. Then I listen to Him."

"Aw, come on now! God doesn't talk to people like that," Tom objected.

"He does through the Bible. Sometimes He sends messages I need through books others have written too."

"Like what?" Tom asked.

Rose opened her Bible and took out a 3 x 5 card.

"One morning I read, 'Do not gratify the enemy by dwelling upon the dark side of your experience; trust Jesus more fully for help to resist temptation. If we thought and talked more of Jesus, and less of ourselves, we should have much more of His presence. . . . All trials that are received as educators will produce joy [Ellen G. White Comments *S.D.A. Bible Commentary*, vol. 4, p. 1183].'

"The ALL seemed too big. I couldn't grasp that. But I copied the sentence on a card and tucked it into the cover of my Bible, asking God to keep me from being depressed and downcast."

"But didn't the constant disapproval from your mother get to you?" Tom asked.

"It surely did. I struggled with guilt for disobeying her. I felt no one understood but Jesus.

"One Friday evening my mother confronted me, 'Tell me. Are you going to obey me or this Jesus?'

"I'm sure my voice shook from fear as I answered, 'I will obey you in every way I can, but I must obey Jesus first.'

"As I told you, my mom's a large, strong woman. At that time I weighed only about ninety pounds. She was so angry she seemed insane. She struck me in the mouth with her fists again and again. Cursing, she continued the blows. She ignored the deep cuts and blood that gushed from my lips. Only exhaustion made her stop. When she dropped into a chair, I ran to the kitchen, holding my head over the sink till the bleeding stopped. Then with a wet washcloth over my mouth, I walked past her to my room. You may be sure, I didn't sleep much that night.''

''Were you in terrible pain?''

''Believe it or not, the next morning when I tried to eat and drink, I felt no pain. But when I looked into the mirror I saw a horrible-looking mouth, swollen like the snout of a pig. I struggled between resentment and forgiveness. But finally I remembered how Jesus never contended for His rights and how He was opposed at home. He gave me the peace of forgiveness. I dressed in my school clothes. This was my day of worship, and I wanted to be with others who loved Jesus.''

''But how could you keep from hating your mother for what she did?''

''Because I kept thinking about Jesus and how He suffered too. Surprised at the joy in my heart, I boarded the bus. As I rode, I opened my Bible and again read the quotation, 'All trials that are received as educators will produce joy.' Now I understood. Jesus does keep His promises, especially when we suffer.''

''I don't think that that promise is for me,'' Tom said.

''But when you get to know Him, He'll help you feel peace even when you hurt,'' Rose answered. ''When I got to church and joined in singing with my swollen lips, I really meant the words of the opening song, 'Praise Him, Praise Him.' ''

''How long did it take for your lips to heal?''

''Just a few days, and look, there are no scars!''

''About this time Christian meetings began at Singapore's downtown Victoria Memorial Hall. Because I wanted so much to know this God who could lift my despair, I attended as many of the meetings as possible. Each night I faced cursing, slapping, threatening.

''However, my inner turmoil did not stop. Each day's new

struggles added to my feeling of helplessness. The situation at home seemed hopeless. I seemed unable to cope.

"One evening Mom stationed herself in front of the one main door to our apartment. When I saw her standing there, I slipped out to the veranda to think. Should I obey her or God? I chose God. Quickly I climbed over the wall into the neighbors' yard. I dashed through their house without a word and hurried to the meeting. All through the meeting I prayed, trying not to think about what would happen when I got back home.

"When I arrived, I breathed a prayer for help and then opened the door to face my mother, whose eyes blazed with anger."

"Not again," Tom groaned.

"Yes, she demanded I give up my Christian ideas, obey her, and serve the gods of our family."

"You really faced a tough situation, didn't you?"

"I really did. I loved my mother. I told her I'd obey her in everything, but God came first. I could no longer worship the Buddha in our living room.

"She became furious. She grabbed my neck with both hands and began to squeeze. I fought for air but could get none."

"Did you think she'd kill you?" Tom raised up on his elbow.

"Yes, I thought I was going to die. I wanted to live, but strangely I felt no fear. Instead, I had an overwhelming desire to pray for my mother. In my thoughts I asked God to forgive her for what she was doing. I know that it sounds unreal, but I can remember an overwhelming sense of peace come over me. Before everything went black, I prayed again, 'Jesus, Thy will be done.' I thought of Jesus returning with His angels. I seemed to enter a dreamlike state, thinking of the sound of the trumpet that would awaken the dead. Suddenly I felt a mighty shove, and I was thrown onto my bed."

"But what made your mother release her stranglehold?" Tom asked.

"I don't know. Maybe an angel. I heard no sound, nor did I see any struggle, but I did see my mother flee from the room. I did sense the presence of God.

"As my strength returned, I thanked God over and over for life. His mighty hands saved me. You see He kept another promise I had recently discovered. He gave it long ago, but He gave it just for me. Listen. 'He saved them from the hand of him that hated them, and redeemed them from the hand of the enemy [Psalm 106:10].' "

"Wow! That's neat! And did the enemy give up and leave you alone after that?" Tom asked.

"Not yet. My family called me stubborn. They begged me to compromise to make Mother happy. Even some of my Christian friends reminded me that the Bible says to honor your parents.

"But I'd fallen in love with Jesus, and I couldn't forget His words, 'He that loveth father or mother more than me is not worthy of me. . . . He that taketh not his cross, and followeth after me is not worthy of me [Matthew 10:37, 38].' "

"You know, Rose, your messed-up life is one kind of cross. Maybe," Tom hesitated, "just maybe my messed-up body is my cross. I wonder if God has plans for me too?"

"I'm sure He does. Following God's plans gives meaning to life's messes."

"How did your messes take on meaning?"

"When I chose to become a Christian, I discovered a new power in my life. God gave me forgiving love with which to reach out to my mother. Somehow she began to accept me. At the next Buddhist festival, without my even asking, she prepared special food for me to eat that hadn't been offered to idols. You see, Tom, when God begins to heal relationships, as well as bodies, He begins from the inside."

Tom looked up at the ceiling. Then, as if discovering a new idea, he muttered, "So—even good people get burned."

Chapter 5

The next few days Rose had only time for a quick ''Hi'' or a wave as she passed Tom's room.

Could her added duties have some connection with the snide remark of the blond nurse who met her coming from his room?

''Why do you talk so much with the patients? Haven't you been told your job is to run errands for us?''

Rose began to feel nervous every time she came in contact with that nurse. Maybe that's why, when carrying a tray with several water containers, she tripped on a cord and dropped everything.

''Clumsy!'' the nurse snorted as she passed her. ''Can't you do anything right?''

The chaplain who had been visiting the patient leaned over as Rose cleaned up the mess on the floor and asked, ''Could you stop by my office when you're off duty this afternoon?''

''I think I could,'' she answered.

And when she did, he welcomed her with a smile.

''Rose, I'm aware of the hassle the nurses are giving you for your interest in the patients. From my viewpoint I think you are contributing to their healing as much with your kind words and prayers as they are with their professional care.''

''Oh, chaplain, I needed that. Today I felt again like a complete failure.''

''What do you mean, again?''

''Oh, I have a history of failures. About the time I became a

Christian I was studying for the difficult Senior Cambridge examination in Singapore. I had to write eight papers covering all the subjects I had taken in high school. Because my family was poor, I used much of my studytime for work. Lots of Singapore students fail these London exams because of their poor English. I feared I would, too, so I prayed constantly for help.''

''But when the results were published, I had failed two of the eight—English and biology. This meant another year of studying, because I had to retake all eight subjects. A year later, I sat for the same exams. My best wasn't good enough. Again I felt the pain of failure. I couldn't understand why. I had tried to follow God in every way I knew, yet He had said No to my earnest prayers.''

''Did you blame God for your failure and disappointment?''

Rose smiled. ''God gave me understanding teachers who allowed me to attend college without a Senior Cambridge certificate. True, I couldn't receive a diploma, but I gained the knowledge. They offered me two jobs, school janitor and work in the registrar's office, to pay my tuition. They even helped me get a scholarship from the mission. You can't imagine my joy when I enrolled in the Bible-training course.''

''How did you find time to study?'' he asked.

''I studied on the bus as I traveled through the city as well as late at night. But I'm sure it was that early hour before dawn with Jesus that gave me the help I needed for each day. My last two years of college I received no financial help, but God supplied jobs so I could pay my bills.''

''So you completed college?''

''Without a degree. They asked me to be the chaplain's assistant at Youngberg Memorial Hospital in Singapore.''

''Interesting. Now I'm beginning to understand your success with the patients. With whom did you work?''

''People of many nationalities come to the hospital—Chinese, Indians, Malays, Europeans, Eurasians, and American. The rich as well as the poor responded to God's love. But many were too sick to comprehend the promises of God. How I wished I could relieve their physical suffering so I could give them spiritual help.

As time went by, I felt I must become a nurse. Yet one great obstacle stood in my way.''

''You mean you had to pass the Senior Cambridge examinations to enter nurses' training?'' the chaplain asked.

''Right. I struggled and prayed about the idea for two years before I decided to try again. Then, four nights a week for one year, I went back to school after working hard at the hospital all day. I tried to do my part by studying every spare moment. I trusted that God would do His part and bring to my mind all I had learned on the days of examination. Surely, I thought, this was His will, for I could widen my field of service for Him. But my plans must not have been God's plans, for I failed the third time.''

Rose paused. The painful memory reopened a wound she thought had healed. She tried to fight back the tears, but they trickled down her cheeks.

''Rose, I've learned that when God allows temporary failures to come, it's because He sees it is best for us and His cause to refuse even our best intentions. Have these failures ever proved a blessing to you?''

''Oh, yes. To preserve my self-worth, I had to depend more on Jesus' love, and His love spilled over to my patients and my family. My mother and I became very close. God didn't grant my desire to pass the exams, but He did give me a greater gift of love and a new kind of service. I'll tell you about that another time. There's something that's bothering me right now on the same subject.''

''And what is it?'' he asked.

''The hospital has offered to send me to school so I can study psychology of nursing, a requirement for the state board exams. They'll pay my fees if I pass with a B grade. But that old fear of failure haunts me. You know my English still isn't good. What if I don't understand the instructors and fail again?''

The chaplain opened his desk drawer. ''For years I've treasured this quotation. Maybe this is a message for you too. Listen: 'Some God trains by bringing to them disappointment and apparent failure. It is His purpose that they should learn to master difficulties. He inspires them with a determination to prove every apparent failure a success. . . . If they will hold the beginning of their confidence steadfast unto the end, God will make their way clear. Success will come as they struggle against apparently insurmountable difficulties, and with success will come the greatest joy [*Gospel Workers*, p. 269].' "

Chapter 6

The night after her visit with the chaplain, Rose enjoyed a quiet talk with each of her children while sitting on the edge of their beds. When she returned to clean up the kitchen, Andrew was just putting the cleanser under the sink. He had polished the faucets till they sparkled, and the sink looked spotless.

"What would I do without you, Andrew!" Rose hugged him impusively. "You do chores most men would never dream of doing. What a super bargain I got when God refused what I asked for and gave me you instead."

"Now just what do you mean, Rose?"

Andrews looked down at his diminutive wife as if he had never heard this before.

"I talked with the chaplain today. I told him about my three failures to pass the Cambridge exams. But I didn't tell him about the better plan God worked out for me."

"You mean when our friend Peter wrote me in Hong Kong about the girl he'd met who was the chaplain's assistant?"

"Yes. I'll never forget that first letter you wrote to me in perfect Chinese characters and how I had to get out a Chinese-English dictionary to read it."

"I had to do the same thing when I got your English letters."

"I always wondered why you took an interest in me when your parents had already arranged for you to marry a pretty girl from Macao."

"I guess I got the feeling that she was more interested in getting a husband than she was in Jesus. The Holy Spirit must have raised questions in my mind about the genuineness of her commitment to Christ. God timed things perfectly, didn't He? Because it was just at this time that Peter wrote about you. He stressed that you loved Jesus so much that it showed in all you did. I liked that. I still do."

Andrew winked at Rose. He liked her bubbly, impulsive ways, so different from his retiring personality.

"As we corresponded I could see that your thoughts, your plans, your decisions all centered in God. I knew you were the girl for me. That's why I made up that parable I wrote you."

Rose laughed. "That parable really puzzled me. It took me a long time to figure out what you meant. Tell me the parable again, Andrew. I always love to hear you tell it."

Andrew took his wife's hand and led her to the sofa. She snuggled into his arms and waited. This had become a ritual in their home. She loved to listen to his quiet voice and feel again the same thrill of love that began that day years ago. But now their love reached deeper and glowed brighter. Both were so engrossed in each other that they didn't hear Joseph go to the bathroom nor did they see him standing in the hallway listening.

Andrew began, "A certain man had just twenty dollars. That was all he had. He could not do his work in bare feet. He needed shoes, for the way had many sharp stones and rough places. Going to the first shop, he saw many shoes. He looked a long while. One pair, made of delicate, beautiful workmanship, especially attracted him. He tried them on. They fit just fine. The price was right. He examined the leather closely. Would they last? Could they stand the rough gravel and the stones? Though beautifully designed, the leather did not look durable. He hesitated. Maybe he should put them aside and look further.

"At the next shop he found another pair, attractively styled, but not as intricately tooled. The price was the same, all he had. They fit comfortably. He spent a long time examining the leather, noting the good quality. The more he looked at this pair of shoes, the more attractive they became. He knew these shoes would endure many long journeys over very rough roads. They had quality that would last to the journey's end.''

Andrew looked down at Rose and smiled. Then he continued, ''I'm glad I gave all I had, my heart of love, to the one who will endure until Jesus comes. God led me to pass up the pretty, delicate pair of shoes, for that which is even more beautiful after years of wear.''

He bent down and kissed her cheek. Just then Joseph sneezed. Both parents turned quickly. There stood their pajama-clad thirteen-year-old with a sheepish grin on his face.

''Dad, what are you talking about? Did you just buy a new pair of shoes?''

''No, Son,'' Andrews said with a laugh. ''I made my purchase fifteen years ago. Those shoes represent your mother. I wrote her that story a long time ago, before I ever saw her.''

''You did? I've often wondered how you and Mother got together when you lived so far apart.''

''Come and join us, Joseph. I think you ought to know how God directed in our lives. Here, sit beside me,'' he said.

Andrew and Rose made room for their son on the sofa. Rose smiled at her tall teenager.

''You'll be amazed, Joseph, how God poured His blessings on us when we trusted His guidance. On my twenty-eighth birthday I received a letter from your dad suggesting that he come to Singapore to discuss marriage. But a few days later he found out the government wouldn't let him enter Singapore. You see, Daddy had fled from mainland China, so he didn't have a Hong Kong passport. So he asked me to come to visit him in Hong Kong.''

''I was afraid your mother wouldn't accept my round trip ticket to fly alone to Hong Kong,'' Andrew added. ''It's not the Chinese custom for the girl to come to the man.''

''Were you afraid, Mother?'' Joseph asked.

''Yes. Sort of. I'd lived only on little Singapore island. Flying alone across the ocean to meet a stranger terrified me. But when my mother consented, God gave me the courage. I experienced a mixture of loneliness and excitement as I boarded the jet. And then, when we met at the Hong Kong airport, we discovered that we couldn't talk to each other.''

"What do you mean, you couldn't talk to each other?'' Joseph looked puzzled.

"The English I'd studied wasn't conversational English. I couldn't understand her, so we tried Chinese. But that didn't work either, for Mother spoke Mandarin and I spoke Cantonese—one of the few dialects she couldn't speak,'' Andrew explained. "I'll never forget those first awkward moments. But love found a way. Before we left the terminal, we found we could do quite well understanding each other, even though we spoke different dialects.''

"Well, I'm sure glad you talk the same language now,'' Joseph said.

"Yes. And I'm glad we can share our memories with you, Joseph,'' his dad continued. "I still feel the joy of that day when I introduced your mother as my bride-to-be to my fellow teachers at South China Union College. Even my skeptical parents were soon convinced God had brought the right two people together.''

Rose's smiling brown eyes, rimmed with glasses, sparkled with love, a deep mature love for God and a vibrant love for the man who held both her hand and her heart.

"Daddy helped ease the loneliness I felt in leaving my mother, all my friends, everything dear to me. Then God gave me you, and a year later Yvette. Babies help fill the emptiness. But I always felt guilty for moving so far from my mother, for I couldn't keep my promise to care for her in her old age. Then God put into Daddy's mind an idea to make my unfulfilled dream come true.''

"What dream?'' Joseph leaned forward with interest.

"To become a nurse. If your dad hadn't been willing to do much more than his share of work, this could never have been. Andrew, please tell Joseph why your thinking is so different from other Chinese men who absolutely refuse to do household work.''

"Well, Son, the Bible says husband and wife should be one. To me that means equality. I'd finished college; Mother hadn't. When I found out she could take nursing in Hong Kong without a

Cambridge certificate, I suggested that I'd stay with you kids while she started prenursing classes at the college. We lived right on campus, you know. We planned a tight schedule so that I could keep my work in the business office up-to-date and meet my deadlines, while she attended classes."

"But Daddy faced ridicule and criticism, especially from his mother, for doing the housework, the cooking, and taking care of you children. I felt guilty for causing all the problems. Were you angry, Andrew, when people insinuated you were henpecked?"

Joseph looked at his father intently, waiting for his answer.

"Why should I? You know I like to cook Chinese food—learned it from my father, who was a chef. Playing with you children relaxed me after a hard day in the office."

"But, Dad," Joseph interrupted, "I'd think you'd get tired of the mess and the crying kids."

"Son, when you love someone the way I love your mother, washing, sweeping floors, or even changing diapers turns a duty into a privilege. Let people talk. I had the approval of Jesus and the joy of seeing Mother happy, and that is what counts.

"But what did you do when Johnny was born?" Joseph insisted.

"He did complicate matters. Mother had finished her prenursing. We had a break till she started training at the hospital in June. But, unfortunately, I couldn't leave Clear Water Bay until September."

Rose took the story up. "So I decided to quit. I couldn't bear to leave you children, but your father wouldn't let me quit," Rose added. "You see, I had about an hour's bus ride to the hospital from the college, but the rules said I had to stay in the nurses' dorm five days a week for those first few months."

"Wow, that must have been tough on you, Dad!"

"It was," Andrew admitted. "Even with baby-sitters to help, I barely managed. Mother spent her weekends picking up the pieces. About that time I'm sure God impressed the hospital managers to ask me to be administrative assistant. We moved into an apartment close by, so Mommy was with us again each day."

"During those busy days of training, Dad often had to be both father and mother to you children," Rose added. "I'd get so lonesome for my family. Many days I only saw you children at lunchtime. How I hated leaving you with baby-sitters, but there was no other way." Rose felt a pang of regret at her loss.

"Yes. And good baby-sitters were hard to find," Andrew remembered. "The first four stayed only a short time. We told God of our great need, and He sent Mrs. Tan. Remember her, Joseph? She loved you as if you were her own boy."

"Sure do. She'd take us for walks, play with us, tell us stories, and never leave us till you or Mother got home."

"She seemed like one of our family those three years till Mother graduated," Andrew added. "Remember your terrible asthma attacks, Joseph? Many nights Mother stayed up with you so I could sleep. Then the next day she'd fall asleep in her nursing classes. To make matters worse, the nursing supervisor threatened to expel her if she went to sleep again in class."

"That's when we clung to the promise, 'If God be for us, who can be against us [Romans 8:31]?' " Rose added. "If only she had let me explain. I remember holding you for three nights, fearing each gasp for breath would be your last. But God kept you alive. He knew we'd reached our limits of endurance, and He helped you sleep the fourth night." Rose sighed, thinking of the exhaustion and relief she'd felt.

Andrew continued, "Each morning before I left for the office and Mother for the hospital, we'd repeat together the promise, 'I can do all things through Christ who strengtheneth me' [Philippians 4:13, NKJV]. Though Mother worked hard and missed much sleep, God kept her well and strong."

"But if Jesus hadn't lifted our burdens, we'd never have made it," Rose added. "Like the supervisor's unreasonable demand that I attend the dormitory assembly each evening instead of our family time of stories and prayer. Again, Daddy had to take my place."

"I liked our storytime, Dad. You always reminded us to pray for Mother," Joseph said.

Andrew looked at the floor as he remembered these events. "So many tried to discourage your mother. She faced constant criticism for neglecting her family. It's a lonely life, constantly being misunderstood. Many urged her to quit."

"But you didn't, Andrew. Not once during those first nine years of our marriage did you complain of the heavy load you had to bear. Our struggles drew us closer together, and closer to Jesus." Rose beamed at both her husband and son.

"Do you recall that special night, Joseph? You were seven years old at the time. I had three-year-old Johnny on my lap, and you and Yvette sat on either side of me. We watched Mother's nursing graduation and felt as if we were graduating too."

"I sure do, Dad. I kept looking from your face to Mommy smiling at us. But I wasn't aware until tonight how you and Mom had struggled together. I remember those years as happy ones."

"That's because God gives peace and joy that's not affected by circumstances," Andrew said. "He took Mother's apparent failure and turned it into tremendous success. Never forget, Son, that with God unanswered prayers and disappointed hopes can become great blessings."

Chapter 7

During lunch break at the hospital, Rose found an empty chair at a table for six. The group chatted as they ate. One of the nurses commented, "My, the hospital seems crowded. I work on surgical floor, and there's not one bed left!"

"That explains why several surgical patients have been placed on our orthopedic section," Amy, an LPN, spoke up. "I've spent the last hour with a cancer patient who is recovering from surgery. The head nurse sent me to cheer her up. She's terribly depressed. Can't say I blame her for crying. Her future looks so hopeless. Several operations, all the radium treatments she can endure, and still they continue to find new lumps. No wonder she's filled with fear."

"What room is she in?" Rose asked.

"Down at the end of the hall, 398," Amy responded. "Rose, you seem to know how to help people. Maybe you could bring her out of the glooms she's in."

"I don't know how to help people in deep depression, but I can ask God to work through me. Is she a Christian?"

"I think so. She has a Bible on her bedside stand. When I left her to come to lunch, she seemed to be approaching hysteria. I called a nurse to stay with her while I took my break."

Amy stood up and picked up her tray. "Please excuse me. I need to get back to my patients," she said.

One by one the others finished their lunches and left. Rose sat alone, thinking as she ate. How would she feel if she had terminal cancer? How could she cope with the fear and the pain? How does one bring hope to a tortured, suffering mind? And then, she remembered one of her favorite promises.

"For I know the thoughts that I think toward you, says the Lord, thoughts of peace and not of evil, to give you a future and a hope." Jeremiah 29:11, NKJV.

As she rode the elevator to third floor, she determined to find an opportunity to bring fresh water to the patient in 398. Maybe God would show her how to give peace and hope. But the incessant demands for her services left no breaks. And now it was three o'clock, time to go home.

Just as she was about to insert her time card into the clock, Amy came up.

"Could you take a minute to see my cancer patient, Rose? She needs your kind of love."

"I hadn't forgotten, Amy, but I've been so busy."

"I know. I've heard you being paged."

Rose turned and walked to the other end of the hospital hall. What could she say to a stranger? What should she do?

She stepped into the room quietly. The patient lay on her side with her face buried in a pillow. Sobs shook her body. Rose waited a moment, praying. Then she heard, between the sobs, muffled words.

"I feel so alone. If only someone would touch me."

Instantly a text she'd so often used as chaplain's assistant flashed into her mind.

"Fear not, for I am with you; be not dismayed, for I am your God! I will strengthen you, I will help you, I will uphold you with my true right hand." Isaiah 41:10, Smith-Goodspeed.

That was her answer. The touch of God's hand through hers might take away fear and bring peace.

Rose said nothing, but reached for the trembling hand. She held it lovingly. With her other hand she gently rubbed the tense neck muscles. With sympathetic love she patted the hand she held or rubbed the damp, hot forehead. That was all.

Slowly the sobs subsided, the tenseness left. The hand she held relaxed. Rose leaned close and whispered, ''May I pray for you?'' she asked.

The patient nodded. Rose held both the patient's hands while she talked to her Lord.

''My Father, You promised to walk with us through the valley of the shadow of death. You told us not to fear evil, for You are with us. With You so close, we can feel Your comfort and strength. We know You alone can give us peace. Help my new friend to keep her mind on You. As she thinks about You, take away her fears. Teach her to trust You. Thank You, in the name of Jesus our Good Shepherd. Amen.''

As Rose continued to rub the patient's neck and back, she repeated softly several times the words from Isaiah 26:3 (NKJV): ''You will keep him in perfect peace, whose mind is stayed on You, because he trusts in You.''

The patient began to breathe slowly and deeply.

''Do you feel like you could go to sleep now?'' Rose asked.

''I think so,'' the patient said as she yawned.

''Just think of yourself resting in the arms of Jesus. He'll hold you close, for He promised He would never leave you. I'll drop by for a short visit before bedtime.''

Rose tiptoed from the room. She hurried home, glad she lived close to the hospital. All three children had reached home before she did.

Yvette met her at the door with, ''Mom, why are you so late? Johnny took my new box of crayons, and he broke the tips off of three of them. He needs a spanking. I wish you'd give him one.''

''I'll settle your squabble later,'' Rose said. ''Right now we all need to work together to have supper ready by the time Daddy gets home.''

After they had eaten, Rose turned to Andrew.

''Will you supervise the cleanup tonight? I promised to visit a very sick patient before bedtime. The charge nurse told me the patient's husband had to be out of town on urgent business. She needs a friend right now who cares. I don't think I'll be gone long.''

"Sure will. Things will be spick and span when you return."

"Thanks lots." She smiled. "And, Johnny, if Yvette had broken the tips off your crayons wouldn't you think it only fair for her to replace them with good ones from her box?"

After a long reflective pause, Johnny admitted, "I guess so," and handed over his box of crayons for settlement.

Rose found the patient propped up with pillows. She seemed to be waiting. Her eyes looked tired, but Rose detected no trace of fear and despair.

"I'm glad you came. Thank you for leaving your family to come to see me tonight. I need to talk to someone who cares," she said.

"I wanted to come." Rose smiled.

"Do you mind if I talk about this depression and fear that overwhelms me? In my weakness, I'm unable to fight my emotions. At such times, only someone, like my husband, who understands and cares, can help me work out of these periods of deep depression. But he had to be gone for several days. You have no idea how your words of comfort soothed my mind and brought me peace."

"They weren't my words. God gave them to me. Jesus is able to do more than we ask or even think," Rose said.

"Well, He certainly used you to do the only thing that could break this iron grip of depression."

"I don't understand. Would you mind explaining?" Rose asked.

"Well, you see, at such times my mind seems confused. I can't think. Part of my mind wants desperately to be happy, to be released from depression. But at the same time I enjoy my self-pity. I want people to understand and sympathize with my misery. My thoughts go round and round like an ugly merry-go-round, pounding in fear and dread. When someone pushes on me words such as, 'Cheer up. Lots of other people have cancer too, and they are worse off than you are,' then the part of my mind that enjoys the depression becomes angry."

"Did the nurses do that?" Rose asked.

"Yes, some of them did, and I felt like screaming at them, 'You don't understand. I'm hurting, and you can't feel how terrible it is.

You can be cheerful, because you don't have cancer. You're only saying words. You don't really care.' So I tuned them out and didn't really hear what they said. Though I really wanted to be released from my depression, my desire for sympathy overpowered everything. I needed someone like my husband, someone who honestly cared. And your tender touch did just that.

"Amy had told me about you and how you showed honest concern for the patients. I hoped you would come, and I recognized you by your accent. But your touch of love—that's what made the difference. Like my husband, you kept showing me that you cared. You didn't give up."

"If you felt better it is because I learned how to treat sick people from my Friend, Jesus," Rose answered. "I have my ups and down too, but He's never given up on me. Like a downpour of rain, He showers me with love. Finally I forget myself and accept His precious gifts of joy and peace. He understands when I'm too wrapped up in myself to accept what I really want. I know He sympathizes with our weaknesses. He sends His angels to comfort us."

"Well this afternoon He used you instead of an angel," the patient interrupted. "And I'm glad you used my favorite psalm in your prayer. When you reminded me that the Good Shepherd was near, I felt secure and unafraid."

"That's beautiful!" Rose beamed. "Isn't it great how Jesus changes everything! When He's near, fear goes and peace takes over. We feel better physically too. I've found my weakness change to strength and hope. I'm so glad you chose to accept God's blessings. It's no fun to wallow in self-centered thoughts."

"I like your honesty. Though I hate to admit it, I'm sure my feelings of self-pity lead to depression. But how, when I'm in pain, can I take my attention from myself?"

Rose did not answer right away. She remembered how many times she had cut off the channel to God by her own selfish thoughts. Finally she said, "My trouble has been that sometimes I've mixed faith with feeling, when really they're as far apart as the east is from the west. Only as I focus on Jesus can I forget self.

That's the first step on the road to recovery from depression.''

"But how? Please be specific." The patient looked perplexed.

"I can only tell you what has helped me whenever I've been depressed. I begin listening to God's own words by repeating over and over in my mind His promises. You can't imagine how quickly the dark feelings melt away, like sunshine breaking through the clouds. Then I feel so good I want to sing." Rose smiled as she remembered.

"You mean there's power in just thinking about the promises of God, that making them personal, really believing they are for me, can take away my bouts with depression?"

Rose saw a ray of hope in the patient's tired eyes.

"May I answer your question with a promise from One whom you can trust?"

The patient nodded.

Rose took the Bible from the bedside stand and read 2 Chronicles 15:7 (NIV): "But as for you, be strong and do not give up, for your work shall be rewarded."

"And it is work, hard work, not to give up," the patient said with a sigh. "Many times during this past year when I've suffered from both the cancer and the radium treatments, I've wanted to die. Please read that verse again. I need to listen carefully to what God is saying to me."

She raised up on one side, placed her elbow on the bed, rested her head on her hand, and listened intently as Rose read again: "But as for you, be strong and do not give up, for your work shall be rewarded."

Looking past Rose, staring into space, she mused for a few moments, then she relaxed back onto her pillow. Minutes passed in silence. Then she spoke with deliberation.

"I think I understand what God is telling me. He knows that depression affects my entire body. It makes my nerves tense. Breathing becomes difficult. Pain increases. I can't eat or sleep. Depression is another form of suicide, slower perhaps, certainly more painful, but suicide nevertheless. On the other hand, if I trust in the Lord for strength and depend on Him, He takes control of my mind. He calms my nerves and fills my mind with positive, cheerful thoughts that react on my body. Thus it's better able to fight the cancer.''

"It may encourage you to know that even Jesus had to depend on a power outside of Himself," Rose added. "He said, 'I can of mine own self do nothing.' [John 5:30]. The trouble is we always want quick answers to every question and easy solutions to every problem. We dislike facing the fact that because we live in this sinful world, we will face situations for which there are no answers or solutions that are acceptable.''

"And then God sent you. Rose, your unhurried presence, your warm, loving heart and open ears became God's answer and solution.''

The woman reached out for Rose's hand.

"Thanks for giving me support and understanding, for letting me lean on you.''

"Just remember Jesus needed love and understanding, too, when He was here on earth," Rose assured her. "He went to His friends three times in the Garden of Gethsemane, longing for words of sympathy and comfort. If only they had understood and appreciated His suffering. Just think how much easier would have been His struggle.''

The cancer patient smiled her contentment.

"That makes me feel better. Now I see that to need and minister to each other isn't to need God less. Oh, how I hope God lets me live. Maybe I can become a channel for giving His love and power to others who have suffered as I have.''

Chapter 8

About two weeks after Rose had her visit with the chaplain, Tom was transferred to a rehabilitation center where they would teach him to walk again. During this time, Rose wavered in her decision to go back to college again. Many factors held her back. She treasured the afternoons and evenings with her family. Should she sacrifice these for class and study? Would it be a good idea to restrict her life into a tighter schedule—going to work, hurrying home, rushing through the housework, delegating much of it to her family, meeting class appointments, along with long hours with her books?

And then, what if she did all that and failed? The hospital had agreed to pay her tuition if she passed with a B. If not, she must pay them back.

One evening after supper Andrew announced, "Could we wait with the dishes? I think we need a family meeting. Let's go into the living room and talk."

Rose guessed Andrew had made a decision. How she loved this kind man who cared so deeply. She noticed how the children listened to his quiet voice.

"We all know of Mother's desire to become a registered nurse. We also know that she is afraid that the burdens will be too much for us. The class she needs begins soon, so she must decide. I'm wondering if you'd like to help her. Would you be willing to play less and do some of the work that Mother does, so she can study?

Will you work with me and be my helpers if Mother goes to school?''

"But, Andrew," Rose interrupted, "you've been talking about going to night school to improve your English, so you'd be eligible for a job in business. I think your future should be considered before mine."

"I'm content with my job. Mechanical drawing is a challenge. Besides, you know I like to be here in the evenings to help the children with their homework. Arithmetic isn't one of your strong points, but I enjoy math."

"I think I could do the washing by myself," Yvette volunteered. "I can fold clothes and put them away. Mother's been teaching me to iron, too, though I don't do very well on your shirts, Daddy."

"And I can run the vacuum cleaner," Johnny spoke up.

Joseph turned to his father, "Dad, for some time now I've wished I knew how to cook Chinese food. Our unit wants to set up a booth and sell it at the Pathfinder Club fair. If you'll teach me, I'll help cook, but—" he paused. "Are you asking us to stop going?"

"And, Dad, our unit is planning a weekend camp-out in the mountains." Yvette's face looked worried. "I want to go so much!"

"And I'll soon be old enough to join." Johnny didn't want to be left out.

"Can we still go to Pathfinder meetings?" they asked in chorus.

"Of course you can," Andrew replied, "but when you're home you may need to work a bit faster and play a little less. Are we ready to vote? Raise your hands if you're willing to do your part so Mother can study."

All hands went up. Tears filled Rose's eyes as she hugged each one of her precious family.

"Thank you, dear ones," she said. "But I'll need your prayers even more. You'll pray for me every day, won't you?"

So Rose enrolled in the community college, promising the hospital that she'd work another two years, if they paid her tuition.

Just as she feared, the teacher in the class on psychology of nursing talked fast and used words she had never heard before. Rose missed much of what she said. The first night she came home discouraged.

"Andrew, I'll never pass this way. What shall I do?"

"We'll buy a tape recorder. You can sit near the front and record the entire lecture. When you come home, you can, listen over and over until you get it all."

That's just what Rose did. She found the course tough, but the more difficulties she faced, the harder she prayed. Because she had to listen to the lectures over and over again and look up many unfamiliar words, she spent much more time in class preparation than the other students. She also studied from January to June, preparing for the state board in July.

When they posted the results of the final examination, she had passed with a B. Thrilled and grateful, Rose was now eligible to sit for the state boards.

She rushed home with the good news. "Let's celebrate—something for my family who helped me succeed. But first, let's praise God in prayer."

They knelt with their arms around each other, each thanking God that Mother passed.

"I know where I'd like to celebrate," Joseph said. "Let's go to the mountains."

"To the Red Rocks." Johnny began jumping up and down. "Maybe all of us could hike up Ship Rock."

"And we could take a picnic lunch," Yvette added.

"A good idea," Andrew said. "How soon could we get ready, Mother?"

"With everybody helping, I think we could leave in half an hour."

As they drove to the nearby mountain park, Rose chatted happily.

"Since tomorrow's my day off, I'm going to write a long letter to my mother. I've been studying so much I've neglected writing for several weeks. She felt so bad years ago when I failed my

Cambridge exams. I know she'll be happy I passed this class. Now I can tell her that maybe I'll become a registered nurse here in America. I've always wished I could have visited her before we left Hong Kong.

"But we had no money for such a trip at the time," Andrew reminded her. "Later God worked a miracle to provide the air fare for us to come here. Aren't you happy for the close relationship you have with her now?"

"Indeed I am. God completely changed her attitude before I left Singapore to marry you. She even insisted I invite my Christian teachers to her home for Chinese New Year and spent days preparing foods she knew they'd enjoy."

"Let's sing because we're all so happy," Johnny interrupted.

"A good idea. You choose the first song. What'll it be?" Rose asked.

"I've got the joy, joy, joy down in my heart." His brown eyes sparkled.

The family sang together until they saw the familiar giant red rocks stretching up into the blue sky.

"Why don't you climb the rocks while I get the food ready," Rose suggested. "Then after we eat, we can hike the trail to the top of Ship Rock."

She watched her family scramble from rock to rock, as she laid out the picnic lunch. Then she relaxed on the mat, waiting for them to return. The warm sun felt good. She had to express her thoughts of gratitude aloud.

"You're so good, God. How can I say Thank You? Maybe I wouldn't enjoy these sunny days so much if You hadn't stayed so close on the dark ones."

After lunch the family had a great time hiking to Ship Rock. Because the steep places took Rose a bit longer than the rest, they returned to the car just at sunset. The children fell asleep on the way home.

"Didn't we have a good time, Rose?" Andrew reached over to hold her hand as they drove home.

"And all because you gave so much of yourself to begin to

make my new dream come true. You've taught the children so much by your unselfish example.''

''My dear, love wouldn't let me do anything else,'' Andrew replied.

The next morning after the children and Andrew had left, Rose hurried with the housework, hoping to finish her letter before the mailman came. Since she'd never mastered writing Chinese characters, she wrote in English. She knew that as soon as her mother received the letter, she'd telephone Rose's younger sister, Margaret, to come and translate it for her.

Rose wrote several pages, knowing how delighted her mother would be as she shared the details of their family celebration. She had just finished the letter when the doorbell rang.

''Special delivery.'' The man handed her a letter postmarked Singapore.

''Are you Mrs. Andrew Lee?''

''Yes.'' She recognized her sister Margaret's handwriting.

''Please sign here,'' he said.

Her hand shook as she wrote her name.

She dropped onto the sofa with the unopened letter in her hand. Fear gripped her. She forced herself to slit the envelope and take out the paper inside, but she hesitated to unfold it. Margaret had never before sent a special-delivery letter. Why, now?

''God, I need You,'' she breathed. Then she unfolded the letter and read.

''Dear Rose, I'm sorry to have to tell you that Mother died last night from a heart attack. We buried her today. I just returned from the cemetery. . . .''

''Oh, no!'' Rose groaned. ''She can't be dead! It must be a mistake. Mother can't be dead!''

Rose felt numb, cold, confused. She stared at the floor, trying to comprehend what had happened. Over and over she repeated, ''Dead! dead!''

She felt she had to express her thoughts aloud. ''Mother died alone. I wasn't with her. I didn't hear her cry. I didn't hold her hand. I wasn't there to kiss her forehead, to soothe her fears, to comfort her. Have I done wrong—to go so far from my mother? And she hadn't received a letter from me for several weeks. Is my dream to become a nurse making me selfish?''

Through Rose's mind flashed memories of her mother—hard and cruel in her childhood and youth; understanding and friendly in her early twenties; precious and loving in her adult life. Questions of self-condemnation cut into her thinking: ''Did Mother understand why I defied her wishes and gave up Buddhism? Did she know I didn't disobey just to be mean? Was it right to break the Chinese customs and live where I could no longer care for her?''

Rose forced herself to read the letter again, still hoping she had misunderstood its import. How she wished that this terrible fact would go away. But reality forced her to believe. Her mother was dead and buried.

Then she noticed the letter she'd just written, the letter her mother would never read. She could never share the joy of yesterday—never—unless, of course—But Mother had never accepted Christ.

Then the tears came. Pressed down with sorrow, Rose felt her heart would break.

The phone rang. She didn't hear it at first, but the rings persisted. Mechanically she took the receiver off the hook and sobbed out a broken Hello. It was Andrew. He often called during his break, when he knew she was home. She heard him say, ''I'll be home as soon as I can.''

In a short time he opened the door and took her into his arms, asking, ''What happened?''

She pointed to the letter. He read and understood. They cried together, talked a little, and cried again.

''Rose dear, I think this room must be filled with angels sent to comfort us,'' Andrew said. ''Tears blind our eyes, but I know Jesus is here. Let's cling to Him. He gave you forgiveness when your mother didn't understand you. He brought unity between you. He's been impressing your mother's heart—''

''But she died a Buddhist and—'' Rose hesitated, not wanting to voice the big question in her mind.

"Remember how she changed and became very close to you after she had treated you so cruelly." Andrew tried to comfort her. "You saw love and compassion grow in her life. When God counts His children, He considers where each is born and the circumstances of their lives. He desires that all should be saved. He knows the heart. Can't we give our children hope that, although their grandmother sleeps, they will see her again?"

"I know our many prayers for her weren't lost." Rose's faith began to reach up. "Yes, Andrew, I can leave Mother in God's hands. We won't know until eternity how the Holy Spirit spoke to her heart and whether she responded. Even before you came home, I kept thinking of the promise, 'My grace is sufficient for you [2 Corinthians 12:9, NIV].' "

Rose smiled through her tears. Andrew held her close and said, "His grace will not only give us comfort in the lonely months ahead, but His love will become so mingled with our sorrow that He will turn our grief into a more precious relationship with Him. Right now, let's just lean on Him while He heals our hurt and pain."

Chapter 9

Eleven months after the Andrew Lee family had arrived in the United States, Rose sat for her state board nursing examinations. Everyone awakened early on that mid-July morning. Andrew and Rose heard the children moving about.

"Let's invite them to join us for a special time of prayer. They've been part of this whole endeavor, and we need their childlike trust," Andrew suggested.

"Let's do," Rose answered. "How many times Johnny has slipped into my room, stood beside me, patted my hand, and said, "I know Jesus is helping you, Mommy. I asked Him to."

Soon three pajama-clad children climbed onto the foot of their parents' bed. Andrew took his Bible from the bedside stand.

"I'll read just one promise this morning. The prophet Jeremiah had been thrown into prison when God gave Him this message. But God didn't mean it just for Jeremiah and God's people back then. It's for us too. Listen carefully and try to understand what God is telling us today: 'Call unto me, and I will answer thee, and shew thee great and mighty things, which thou knowest not [Jeremiah 33:3].' " Andrew reached for another Bible. "Now I'll read the same verse from the New International Version, a modern translation: 'Call to me, and I will answer you and tell you great and unsearchable things you do not know.' What's God saying to Mother and to us in this message?"

Johnny spoke first. "Maybe God's telling her that when she

comes to questions in her test that she doesn't know, she's to ask Him for the answers.''

"Better yet,'' interrupted Joseph, "I think God will give Mother a keen mind so when she meets difficult multiple-choice questions, she can understand the hidden meaning.''

Yvette, shy and quiet, said, "I hope God is telling Mother she'll pass the state boards if she puts her trust in Him.''

"I think this message has a deeper meaning for Mother than just passing an exam,'' Andrew spoke slowly and thoughtfully. "God knows Mother has done her best to prepare, and He wants her to succeed. But, I think it's only fair that we consider the factors of human limitation. God does not usually give people the ability to understand another language perfectly. This means that should Mother fail, He has not let her down.''

"But doesn't God have our best interests in mind?'' Joseph asked.

"Yes. But we don't always recognize His 'something better' until our plans fail. Whatever the outcome, this could be a tremendous learning experience of great and mighty truths that up until now have been hidden from all of us.''

Rose swallowed hard before she could speak. "Thank you, all of you, for praying that God's will be done and that He will open my mind to see these great, hidden things.''

Then the family knelt and prayed.

After the exam, Rose went about her life with joy, knowing she had done her best, refusing to worry about the results. She was working the three-to-eleven shift on September 21 when she heard the announcement that the results of the National Council Licensing examinations had come. Quickly she went to the designated place to receive her envelope—She had failed!

She stared at the paper in shock. This couldn't be! She checked to see whether they had given her the right envelope. She read it again. Had she been betrayed by God? She remembered how certain she had been of God's presence as she wrote the exam. Had she been deceived? In her bewilderment she forgot what Andrew had said in their early-morning worship. Anger toward God who seemed not to care that her dreams were smashed, temporarily filled her thoughts.

Numbly, she walked back to her floor. She tried to act busy, to collect her thoughts, but everything seemed confused. Then she heard happy voices—others congratulating those who had passed. She fought back tears of disappointment. The happy voices came closer. She knew she must say something.

"I'm glad you passed," she forced herself to say. "Congratulations!"

The hours dragged by. Feelings of resentment and disappointment added weight to the already heavy feeling in her heart. She stood in the hall, feeling disoriented, trying to focus her mind on the tasks at hand, trying to remember what her orders had been.

An older nurse came close, put her arm around her, and whispered, "I'm sorry, Rose, so sorry for your disappointment."

For the first time since the shock of failure, she felt the warmth of human love and sympathy. She tried to respond, to express her appreciation, but words wouldn't come. She bit her lip and looked at the floor.

The nurse patted her shoulder and went to a patient's room.

She knew she couldn't hold out until eleven o'clock without help. Her hurt was too deep. From habit, out of her great need, she cried to God, "Help me, Lord Jesus."

And then she remembered her orders—supply fresh water to the patients for the night. She began in the room where the older nurse had gone.

"I hope you sleep well tonight," she said, without much feeling, to the man in the bed near the window.

"You amaze me," he said. "The nurse told me about your disappointment. How can you keep on going when you hurt so bad inside?"

Even though she still felt shattered, Rose had to speak the truth.

"My Lord Jesus gives me strength. I couldn't keep on without Him, for He sustains me."

"I'm glad you said that." The man smiled. "We sick folks need to see that kind of courage."

These words kept her going until eleven o'clock. She dreaded telling the news to her family. Fortunately, all were asleep except Andrew. She poured out her pent-up emotions on him.

"Why, Andrew, why? God knows how much I want to be a nurse and not just a servant. What about all our prayers, all the promises we claimed? Why did God permit this when I studied so hard and tried to do His will? How can I face my fellow staff members when they know I'm a failure? Why, Andrew, why?"

She burst into tears. Andrew tried to comfort her, tried to explain to her that God never says No unless He has a better plan. He tried to get her to look to Him in faith, but she wasn't listening. She cried until she finally fell asleep sometime just before dawn.

The next morning, Andrew called his employer and received permission to have the morning off.

After the children had left for school, he said, "Rose, please do me a favor. I'd like you to go with me to Washington Park. We could walk and talk in the rose garden."

Rose needed no persuasion. She did not wish to spend the morning alone.

They looked at the beautiful roses a while; then Andrew said, "Tell me, Rose, how do you feel?"

"Resentful. I resent the way the nurses look down on me. I feel like a Chinese *amah*, a servant, just doing menial tasks they feel are beneath them. When we came to America, I took this job because it was all I could find. But each day is more difficult since the nurses constantly take advantage of me because I'm a foreigner. After all, I am a graduate nurse too."

"I'm so sorry." Andrew grasped her hand as they walked. "If only you had told me before."

Rose couldn't stop talking. "I feel as if God let me down. He knows I wanted to do a greater service for Him, to minister directly to the patients, and not just wait on the staff. I've tried to do my work cheerfully, hoping for a change. But now, hope is gone. I'm a failure. Even God can't change that." She paused, and then added bitterly, "or doesn't want to."

"Rose, sometimes there are no logical answers to our questions. When you did so well in your class, we all felt you would pass the boards. I don't know what God is trying to tell you, but I do know He did not cause you to fail.''

They sat down on a park bench facing the roses. Andrew began to sing softly the familiar song containing the line, "I don't know about tomorrow."

Tears flowed down Rose's cheeks as she said, "Andrew, I know God isn't dead, that I serve a living Saviour. I know He loves me. Yesterday I felt angry; today I'm perplexed. On the day of the exams I prayed for wisdom so I could be of greater service to the patients. Does He want me to spend my life running errands any teenager could do? Is my call to service just to wait on the staff? Today I feel like the disciples who cried out in the storm, 'Master, carest thou not that we perish [Mark 4:38]?' ''

"But Jesus did care," Andrew added. "After He had calmed the waters, He asked, 'Why are you so afraid? Do you still have no faith [Mark 4:40, NIV]?' ''

Andrew squeezed her hand.

"Rose, God's viewpoint is far different from ours. When we choose Him, there's no such thing as real failure or defeat. What has happened may seem like a defeat to us, but now's the time to trust God, to believe He allows to happen only that which is for our best good. We'd never learn to sympathize with other's misfortunes, to heal hearts, if we had never experienced pain. How can we understand other's sorrows unless we have known sorrow personally? Maybe today you're taking the real examination, the one that will count for eternity. Remember that God can turn a seeming defeat into a glorious victory. Let's pray together. I'm sure that God will give you peace and trust."

They bowed their heads, and for a time Rose allowed the Master to still the storm in her mind.

That afternoon, as she entered the hospital lobby, she met the husband of one of the nurses. He had recently recovered from a serious illness. Often Rose had stopped by his room to encourage him, to pray with him. He came right to the point.

"My wife told me about your disappointment, Rose,' he said.

"Remember your own words of courage and hope, the promises and prayers you said for me. Now it's your turn to live what you preach."

Rose tried. When she trusted God, she could live above her gloom. But she couldn't seem to forget her failed examination. At such times she became a different Rose. Despair displaced her usual smile. She became resentful of the charge nurse. Why should she do work not assigned to her? Heretofore she had gone out of her way to do what needed to be done, whenever she saw a need, such as making a bed or putting a patient on a bedpan.

Absorbed in these thoughts, she felt rising resentment when a nurse ordered, "Rose, empty the urinal bag in 349."

"Maybe I ought to ask the head nurse if she wants me, the ward assistant, to do nurses' work," Rose shot back. The nurse looked at her in surprise, as if to ask, What's got into *you*?

Rose hurried to the nurses' station and asked if she was expected to do nurses' work when she was only a ward assistant. The head nurse was new and seemed confused. She hesitated and then said, "Well, I suppose it's all right, if the nurse is very busy."

But Rose knew the nurses often claimed to be busy just to slough off onto her tasks they didn't want to do.

"I've never faced a situation as you describe," the new head nurse continued, "I don't think you'd get into trouble. Why don't you talk with Mrs. Crankshaw, the assistant director of nurses. She'd know the correct procedures."

Rose wondered whether she were being given the runaround. She became so absorbed in the problem, she never thought to ask God for guidance and failed to discuss her feelings with Andrew. She carried her burden alone.

Several days later she received an appointment to see the assistant director of nurses. When she entered her office, the director greeted her with a hard look and a snappy "What do you want?"

As she explained, Rose noticed a flush of redness begin to spread from the director's neck and spread across her face.

"Listen," she almost shouted when Rose stopped speaking,

"in the future you are not to come and see me or the personnel director. You take your petty complaints to the head nurse. If she can't settle the problems, she, not you, will come to me. I hope you understand."

Rose understood only too well.

A few evenings later, Rose took a respirator machine to the room of a very ill patient. The woman moaned in pain. Rose stepped over to her bed, leaned over, and whispered, "Is there anything I can do to help you?"

"Yes. Please pray. I hurt so much. Ask God to give me relief so I can sleep."

When she had finished praying, Rose looked up to see an LPN watching her. As she came into the hall, the LPN said in a voice of thunder, "It's not your job to pray for the patients. That's the chaplain's work. Your job is to help us nurses, not the patients."

Fear mingled with resentment haunted Rose. These past two weeks since she'd heard the results and faced failure had been a nightmare. She saw or imagined she saw unfriendly looks. She felt she was being watched, that no one cared about her feelings, that she was alone.

Chapter 10

I saw Rose reach out in love, even as she went through her
Gethsemane. During the time of her deepest depression, she and
Andrew drove across the city to visit my eighty-five-year-old
mother, who suffered from a broken hip. My mother never understood the depth of meaning in the words they sang by her bedside,
"I don't know about tomorrow, but I know who holds my hand."
They gave her some homemade Chinese cookies and chatted happily. Rose and Andrew had come to bring joy, not to add to my
mother's sufferings.

But all the while Rose was learning to understand a bit better
Jesus' agony when, in Gethsemane, He chose to submit to the will
of His Father. She, too, had felt the intense reality of that struggle. She saw some of the depths of the loneliness Jesus passed
through when she had to make certain decisions in the awful loneliness of her own soul.

Could she surrender her dearest plans, her failures, her whole
life to Him? Had she entered heaven through prayer, so she could
face the disappointments of earth? Had she come to the place
where she could even thank God for the gifts of loneliness and
rejection that forced her to reach up to her heavenly Father and
out to others?

Rose had just taken a patient from X ray back to her room when
she met her friend, the chaplain.

"I've been looking for you," he said. "I've been carrying a little card in one of my pockets for several days hoping to see you. Ah, here it is. I think you'll like the message written on it.''

He placed it in her hand and was gone.

Rose read, ''Trust is knowing that whatever God allows to happen in my life is prompted by love.''

At that moment she heard on the loud speaker, ''Rose Lee, head nurse's office.''

Suddenly her mouth seemed as dry as cotton and her heart beat wildly. Her hand shook as she knocked on the door. ''Now what?'' she thought.

''Sit down, Rose. I've called you in for a job evaluation.''

The icy sound in the nurse's voice sent chills down Rose's spine.

''You know, of course, that I've been head nurse on this ward for six weeks. During this time I have received reports that you have shown a negative attitude toward the staff when you've been asked for assistance. You have also communicated negative nonverbal messages to the staff.''

She paused and cleared her throat.

''For the next three months you will be on probation starting today, November 4. During this time, I, as the head nurse, will meet with you every week, to determine whether you have met the following goals. Here they are.'' She picked up a sheet of paper that lay on her desk. In tones heavy with authority she read:

1. You will request assistance from the charge nurses in prioritizing requests from the staff.
2. You will exhibit a more positive attitude toward the staff when asked for assistance.
3. You will try to become aware of the ways in which you communicate negative nonverbal messages.
4. You will seek out ways in which you can offer assistance to the staff.
5. You will work on organizational skills.

She paused to let her words sink in. ''If this probation is not successfully met, termination will follow.''

For several minutes neither said anything. Rose could hear the pounding of her heart. Finally the nurse looked at, or perhaps more accurately, through her. She reached across the desk and handed her the sheet of paper.

"You may have a copy of these goals. I expect you to do your utmost to comply. When you meet with me a week from today, we will discuss your progress, or lack of it."

The nurse stood up in a peremptory manner and gestured her toward the door.

"Now go back to your work," she commanded.

Rose felt like a criminal condemned, without having been given an opportunity to defend herself. But she knew this head nurse would never understand the reasons for her actions. Was no one interested in her viewpoint?

Like a tidal wave, conflicts without and within swept over Rose. It was too much. She felt she could not continue to work in an atmosphere of distrust. Her mind spun in circles—"They insist on misunderstanding my motives—I'm being watched—No one cares—I must get out." The more the problem of her unjust treatment spun in her head, the more the anger, hurt, and frustration increased.

That's why when she met the head nurse at the nursing station the next day, she inquired, "Please, may I ask you a question?"

"Go ahead."

"I'd like to be transferred to work on another floor of the hospital. Please, may I change?"

"All transfers are handled at the staff office, where you make written application," she answered curtly.

Instead of asking for divine guidance, Rose made a snap decision. During her next break, she hurried to the office and asked for an application form. One blank said, "State your reasons for requesting a change."

With naïve honesty, Rose wrote, "Attitude of head nurse."

She doubtless would have been more tactful had she known that all applications were scrutinized by the director of nurses, who had a reputation for dismissing employees who did not comply to the fullest with her wishes.

The next day the charge nurse handed her a note which read:

"Rose Lee, ward assistant. Your application for request to be transferred to another floor will be held in my office during the three-month probationary period. Also, your salary increase will be put on hold during that time. There will be no changes until we can determine whether your probation is successfully met. Other-wise, termination will follow. Ruth Crankshaw, director of nurses."

Rose felt isolated, entangled in a web from which escape seemed impossible. It was obvious that there was no use going to her superiors for help. She couldn't trust the nurses, LPNs, or anyone on the staff. Painfully confused, she stuffed the note into her uniform pocket. And then she felt the card the chaplain had given her. In the stress of the past few days, she'd forgotten he had given it to her.

She read again, "Trust is knowing that whatever God allows to happen in my life is prompted by love."

"Where was love in this hopeless situation?" she wondered. "I think I'll talk with the chaplain," she said to herself. "Maybe he can understand my suffering and hurt."

Instead of going home from work, she first stopped at his office and asked for an appointment.

"The chaplain is free," his secretary said. "Would you like to talk with him now?"

"Please," she said.

But when he invited her to sit down, she couldn't talk; she could only cry. But she did place on his desk two sheets of paper, the probationary demands and the note from the director of nurses.

He read them carefully and then looked out the window, think-ing. Rose's sobs quieted, but still he did not look at her nor speak. Several minutes passed before Rose asked her bitter question, "Why do people reject me? Why do they lack trust and confi-dence in me, when I've tried to do my best?"

"Rose, before we can come to terms with suffering such as you're experiencing, we need to understand two preliminary concepts—sin and freedom. May I digress a bit, before we discuss your question?''

''If it will help.''

''I think it will. You see, Rose, when God gave us freedom, which is the power to choose, evil became possible. Just as freedom makes sin possible, so sin makes suffering possible. The real question is not 'Why did this happen to me?' or 'What did I do to deserve this?' but 'God, why did you make us free?' ''

He continued, ''Often after I've spent hours listening to human tragedy, and believe me I get lots of it in this job, I think, 'God, You put too much faith in us. We've blown it. Look at what we're doing to ourselves.' But God chose to make us free, because only thus could we respond to Him with true love.''

Rose interrupted him. ''But I don't feel free when everyone misjudges my motives. I feel as if I'm on trial! Every disapproval is a new sentence pronouncing me guilty. I can't handle that for three months!''

''I understand,'' the chaplain empathized. ''Right now you feel so threatened and uncomfortable that you want to get away from it all. But I believe that deep inside, you really don't want to escape. Instead of running away from your problem, look for a doorway through it.

''But whatever I do, they'll misinterpret my motives,'' Rose bemoaned.

''I've appreciated your compassion and concern for your patients, Rose. Apparently others have not. Nor have they noticed how you've gone the second mile in helping the nurses. I've wished the staff would make allowances for a foreigner who doesn't understand the protocol of a large hospital, or that they would at least offer suggestions on correct procedures. Surely you've made blunders, Rose, but not intentionally. I wish they could have been overlooked and forgiven.''

Rose smiled, thankful someone appreciated her efforts.

The chaplain reached for a black book on the desk.

''Paul has the answer to the problem of injustice. Listen. 'Love keeps no score of wrongs; does not gloat over other men's sins, but delights in the truth. There is nothing love cannot face; there is no limit to its faith, its hope, and its endurance [1 Corinthians 13:5-7, NEB].'

"That's the way Jesus handled rejection and loneliness. Love is the only way through."

"Yes, I guess I know that, but it's so hard to practice," Rose admitted.

"Would you be willing to change your viewpoint toward those probationary goals? Instead of seeing them as a threat, why not accept the five points as a challenge to change?"

Rose's eyes lighted up. "I've been thinking negative thoughts, and my thoughts have been reflected by my attitude and my actions. But I can choose to change all that!"

"Of course you can! You've been living in fear, building up inner defenses. Now you can be openly honest."

Rose looked out the window for several minutes. Then she faced the chaplain. "OK, I accept the challenge. And you know, I like the thought that what seemed a threat to me, now appears like an open door. I'm so ashamed at the way I've hurt my Jesus!"

Tears filled Rose's eyes. Not tears of self-pity, but tears of repentance and love. She sobbed, "My disappointment got so huge I couldn't see anything else. And then everything in life got out of focus. But you're right. Now I'm free to start over. By God's grace, I'm going to trust Him completely. Maybe someday I shall know that even my failure of the state boards was allowed by His love.

"But, chaplain, I have another problem. I have difficulty with English. You see, the state board of nursing requires that I take the oral test of spoken English. In addition I have to take the written test of English as a foreign language in order to be eligible for next year's licensing examinations. This is not only expensive, but it requires so much preparation. I've requested a waiver since I've had three years of college. What if that's not granted?"

"My faith is simple enough to believe you'll receive the waiver if that is what God sees is best for you. If not, He will make plain what His plan for you is. Rose, in my job as chaplain, I face insurmountable people problems every day. Humanly speaking, they overwhelm me. That's why I placed this quotation under the glass on my desk. Reading it repeatedly lifts me above discouragement and despair. May I share it with you as the door through all your problems—even this one?"

"Please do."

"Then come and follow along as I read."

Rose slipped over to his desk as he read, "Prayer is the answer to every problem in life. It puts us in tune with divine wisdom, which knows how to adjust everything perfectly. So often we do not pray in certain situations, because from our standpoint the outlook is hopeless. But nothing is impossible with God. Nothing is so entangled that it cannot be remedied; no human relationship is too strained for God to bring about human reconciliation and understanding; no habit so deep rooted that it cannot be overcome; no one so weak that he cannot be strong. No one is so ill that he cannot be healed. No mind is so dull that it cannot be made brilliant. Whatever we need if we trust God, He will supply it. If anything is causing worry or anxiety, let us stop rehearsing the difficulty and trust God for healing, love, and power [Ellen G. White, *Review and Herald*, October 7, 1865]. "

Epilogue

Rose and others have found that life's problems usually do not vanish at once. Hurts take time to heal. However, our mental response can drastically change our relationship to even the worst troubles. Through them I've discovered the precious truths from the psalmist who said, "A righteous man may have many troubles, but the Lord delivers him from them ALL." Psalm 34:19, NIV, emphasis supplied. *All* is a mighty big word, but God is big enough to keep His promises.

Since learning this truth I have enjoyed that peaceful excitement of learning to wait on the Lord. I can't do it without a daily supply of grace and patience to endure, while watching God untangle seemingly hopeless situations.

Rose, too, knows what I mean. After those trying three months of probation she received a note from the clinical manager of the hospital which said, "Rose Lee has successfully completed the terms of her probationary period as outlined in the counseling memo of November 4, 1982."

Then came a letter from the consultant of the board of nursing saying, "The board has granted your request for a waiver to take the test of English as a foreign language. You are eligible to take the national licensing examinations without first taking the TOEFL."

Within a few days God opened another door—acceptance to attend summer review classes that would enable her to take the LPN examinations in the fall.

I like the vibrancy in a letter I recently received from Rose. In it she writes, "When I see Jesus face to face, I shall thank Him for loving me so much that He allowed my plans to fail so His could succeed. I'm sure He'll explain why He permits good people to get hurt. Then I'll understand why Jesus permitted me to lose my mother, fail my exams, and endure the rejection and humiliation of three months' probation. Until then, I'll trust my Jesus to help me through life's problems until He comes to take me home."

Tough times come to us all. The hurt, the chagrin, the embarrassment may be anything but fair. But God knows how to compensate, how to shelter the heart from bitterness. He, too, learned all this through personal experience.